S0-CAI-333

A Further Semester

Books by Anne Marx

Ein Buechlein; German Lyrics, 1935
Into the Wind of Waking, 1960
The Second Voice, 1963
By Grace of Pain, 1966
By Way of People, 1970
A Time to Mend: Selected Poems, 1960–1970
Hear of Israel and Other Poems, 1975
Forty Love Poems for Forty Years, 1977
Face Lifts for All Seasons, 1980
Forty-five Love Poems for Forty-five Years, 1982
Holocaust Hurts to Healings, 1984
A Further Semester, 1985

CO-EDITOR:

The World's Love Poetry, Bantam Books, 1960
Pegasus in the Seventies, McClure Company, 1973

A Further Semester

NEW POEMS BY

Anne Marx

1985

William L. Bauhan, Publisher
DUBLIN, NEW HAMPSHIRE

PS3563
.A75
F8
1985

Copyright © 1985 by Anne Marx
All rights reserved
Library of Congress Cataloguing in Publication data:
Marx, Anne.
A further semester
I. Title
PS3563.A75F8   1985   811'.54   84-20433
ISBN   0-87233-078-8

Composed in Bembo type with titles in Perpetua
by A & B Typesetters, Concord, N.H., printed at the
Transcript Printing Co., Peterborough, N.H. and bound
at the New Hampshire Bindery, Concord.

*This book is dedicated
to my true family and friends,
to my fictional family and friends
who are composites of people encountered,
to all men and women whose identities I adopted
in some of these poems*

Acknowledgments

Grateful acknowledgment is due to the editors of the following magazines, newspapers and anthologies in which most of the poems included in this collection appeared within the past two years:

Alura Poetry Quarterly, I, Walt Whitman, Listening; *Back Home in Kentucky*, Himself a Seedling; *Bitterroot*, Two Learned Loving, A Manmade Corsage; *The Country Poet*, In Memory of My Father, Rondeau of Acceptance; *Encore*, A Shock of Green, Summer Chill in New Mexico, A Rushing of Her Seasons, Final Performance, Slum Story; *Eve's Eden* (Anth. India), May Some Islands Dream Awhile; *Eve's Legacy* (Anth. U.S.), Cold Morning Truth; *A Galaxy of Verse*, Behind Barriers of Global Communication, Amputee on the Beach, Recuperation, What Is a Happy New Year?; *Good Housekeeping Magazine*, The Lone Ascent; *Gryphon* (Univ. of So. Florida), Annual Convention, Dear Amy; *Hartford Courant*, Three Haiku For New Spring; *The Inkling Selection, A Poetry Anthology*, With Wagner, Through Storm to Calm; *The Inquirer* (Scarsdale and Greenburgh), Gypsy Moths, Small Courtesies, Storm Damage Redeemed, A Boy's Deliverance; *Japanophile*, Motion and Emotion: Tokyo to Kyoto; *The Lyric*, Departures, A Mutual Gift; *Love Lyrics Anthology*, Geometry of Love; *Poets On*: A Study of L's Work, My Sister Survivor, Day of Deliverance, Small Pickings; *Pomegranate Series of Writers and Readers* 1982, Visitor of Thirteen Springs; *Prize Poems of the Nat. Fed. of State Poetry Societies* 1983, Hands Remember; *Prize Poems, PPS* 1982, My Sonnet is a Subterfuge, *Prize Poems PPS* 1983, Tante Marie: Her Sheltered Existence; *Prize Poems PPS* 1984, My Inviolate Land, *The Study and Writing of Poetry: American Women Poets Discuss Their Craft* (Whitston Publishing Co.), Rondeau for a Friend With an Unalterable Schedule; *The Survivors*, April Recoveries, *Today's Great Poems* 1983 (Anth.) Testament; *Voices International*, Sestina Letter to a Wondrous Strange Son, Spring Cleaning.

"Elegy for the Victims of the Holocaust from Worms" prefaced the book *The Destruction of the Jewish Community of Worms 1933–1945* by Prof. Henry Huttenbach, in English and German, 1981, and has been reprinted in German and American publications. Most of the above poems have also won recent prizes in competitions of The National League of American Pen Women; The World Order of Narrative Poets; The New York Poetry Forum, *The Writer's Digest*, and in poetry contests of various states. Certain poems have been reprinted in *The Pen Woman*.

"In Memory of My Father, Undaunted Country Doctor" was awarded a prize by the World Order of Narrative Poets for its use of the traditional but unusual form, the Greater Sapphic Line.

Contents

I. HISTORY, OLD AND NEW

Hands Remember	11
Himself a Seedling	12
A Boy's Deliverance	13
Letter to a Wondrous Strange Son	15
Visitor of Thirteen Springs	17
Cold Morning Truth	18
My Father, Undaunted Country Doctor	20
My Sister, Survivor	22
Tante Marie: Her Sheltered Existence	24
Reconciliation at a Wedding	25
For My Son's Second Wedding Day	26
A Manmade Corsage	27
The Remarriage	28
A Rushing of Her Seasons	31
With Wagner: Through Storm to Calm	32
Victims of the Holocaust from Worms	33
Between Two Graves, a World Apart	34

II. NATURE AND ART STUDIES

Rondeau of Acceptance	39
Day of Deliverance	40
Storm Damage Redeemed	41
Three Haiku for New Spring	42
April Recoveries	43
A Gift of Freedom from Dandelions	44
Spring Cleaning	45
Gypsy Moths	46
Summer Chill in New Mexico	47
A Shock of Green	48
The Lone Ascent	49
May Some Islands Dream Awhile	50
Motion and Emotion: Tokyo to Kyoto	51
A Study of L's Work	52

For Muriel Rukeyser 54
Villanelle for a Beloved Poet 55
Annual Convention: Eating Your Words 56
Birth Pangs of a New Sonnet 57
My Inviolate Land 59

III. THE NEW ARITHMETIC OF LOVE AND FRIENDSHIP

Geometry of Love 63
Two Learned Loving 64
Breaking Through His Sound Barrier 65
Love Be a Shield 66
My Sonnet is a Subterfuge 67
Dear Amy 68
In Praise of Elizabeth, No Saint 69
Friend with an Unalterable Schedule 70
Behind Barriers of Global Communication 71
Testament 72

IV. THE HUMANITIES: TESTS AND FINALS

I, Walt Whitman, Listening 75
Slum Story 76
Shopping Trip 77
Ballade of the Lad on the Promising Sea 78
The Pocketknife 79
Amputee on the Beach 81
Small Pickings 82
Of Birth and Death on a Kibbutz 84
Departures 87
Coping With Losses: Sequence of Mason Sonnets 88
    A Natural Law 88
    Recuperation 89
    Compensations 90
    That Needed Strength 91
    A Mutual Gift 92
    Final Performance 93
    Final Collection 94
What is a Happy New Year? 95

I

History, Old and New

Hands Remember

I reach for the crocheting hook and cast
the stitches on, my chain increasing fast,
as someone taught me in my German past
decades ago—her shape and voice untraced—
to fashion scarves for soldiers at their post
up at the front. We schoolgirls liked her best
of all our teachers, someone we addressed
as "Fräulein" . . . by what name? One day we missed
her face at a new term, among the rest
who sometimes vanished from our chain. Distressed,
we learned she had been sent away, the last
we ever heard. Now here along the coast
of my new land, I try to pass the test
she never gave . . . an even start a must
for future rows to match from East to West,
a hook in charge, returning West to East
goosestepping line by line. A holocaust
of memory threads is wrapped around my wrist
as hands remember what the brain has lost.

Himself a Seedling

What secret brings about this transformation
of boy to man among forget-me-nots
and primrose, as he moves around the garden
uncradling fragile plants from flower-pots?

How hesitant we were to let him venture
to make this spring-time border all alone,
transplanting annuals he started early —
himself a seedling sprouting on his own.

Remembering broken glass and damaged woodwork,
the nicks in table tops, a springless chair,
we watch amazed those once-so-awkward fingers
at ease now, capable of tender care.

Some day a girl, a slender morning-glory,
will lean upon him sensing sturdy wood.
His gentleness shall hold her as a trellis
for slow unfolding into womanhood.

A Boy's Deliverance

Once in a while
I meet her in the village,
still slim and quick
though long retired now;
formerly jet-black bangs
greying exclamation-marks
above the animated face.
She always asks: How is
Tommy doing? I tell her
that he's doing well, all
thanks to her (long turned
into a Thomas and a first-rate
scholar) She sends her love.

He was in fourth grade when
we were summoned to appear
before the principal.
Tom's teacher, straight-laced,
rigid like her corset, vowed
she could no longer cope
with his defiance. We learned
he spent a lot of classroom
hours in the hall, banished
like a leper. The principal
was an impartial metronome
going from side to side.

Might we decide on private school?

Troubled, at home, another call:
Let's try him in the other
fourth grade class . . .
It was a turning point for all.
Miss Hultz brought out the best
in Tommy, in her land of joyful
learning. Her influence, like a
long-lasting shower, loosened the
soil of his defiance, throughout
the long years of school ahead.
Although she had him only for one year,
she had him, had him at a vital moment.
We never learned her secret.

In vain, I search for a trace
of you where you have lain.
Suddenly old, I reject the cold
morning-truth of never holding
another child of my own,
and never to feed female flesh
and bone with my body. I clutch
at the dream to salvage your fragrance
against my breast that aches with need.

In Memory of My Father,
Undaunted Country Doctor

Carcinoma, scourge of the flesh, vanquish the lurking monster
finding victims heedless of rank, sparing not priest nor gangster,
king or beggar, laborer, bum, president, writer, dancer—
Hail to healers, neither immune, valiantly battling cancer!

Father had some warnings ahead . . . Suddenly feeling weary,
paid no mind to signals that would cause someone else to vary
office hours and strenuous trips, visits to bed-bound patients,
a country doctor devising his own treatments and consultations.

Tests and x-rays, positive proof, now it was time to enter
painful stages, therapy-blurred . . . life could not last through winter.
May and April passed under clouds. May was the month of clearing:
Father left his hospital bed. No one dared interfering . . .

How to count the score of his days? Time was his sole possession.
Many patients needed his skill, hopeful their own condition.
I remember waiting for Dad, walking him home for dinner—
paler, weaker every week, nevertheless a winner.

Hand in hand we managed our hill. Neighbors and friends were hailing
father strangely, reverently, seeing a savior failing.
I, too young for accepting death, firmly believed he'd recover,
somehow trusting miracles could make him remain forever.

Autumn came with menacing skies, muscles no longer moving;
still, he saw some cases at home, tending to them and proving
Man overcomes his suffering self, relieving the pain of his brothers.
Men are living due to my Dad. Following him came others . . .

A doctor died those decades ago. My darkness had come unbidden,
but lights he lit in a cancerous world are never to be forgotten.
Vanish, cancer! Enemy, yield! Healers shall keep assuring
ever greater hope for a sick humanity's final curing!

My Sister, Survivor

By now, she is back in Florida
after the hurried weekend visit North.
Two brilliant July days, we sat talking,
rehearsing our shared past.
Why were our memories not all the same?
("What did father die of," she asked.
"Of cancer, of course," I said.
"No, he died of a broken heart
after mother's death!" That's what
the servants told her, because she was
so young . . . Did she still believe
he lacked the will to live?)

Outside, the breezes ruffled giant maples,
and my hammock beckoned gently.
"Remember our garden in Germany?"
I found a yellowed photograph,
my sister in her carriage under linden trees;
I, big sister, clinging to the handlebars;
mother in a hammock, looking happy,
a year before the epidemic struck.

My little sister, true Floridian,
looks as young as a well-retouched photo,
is apt to flirt and, giggling, pass for forty.
Only that stormy evening she arrived,
I had a shock when her rainhood came off
along with the expensive curly wig
for a brief glimpse of glistening scalp beneath.
She laughed it off.

Now she is back down South
in time for another scheduled treatment,
the chemotherapy that leaves her sick
to make her well. Next year, she said,
her hair would grow more lushly than before.
She left, still laughing.
Our current memories are all the same —
a summer day of new-found knowledge that
our parents might have lived long lives
in our blessed age of modern medicine . . .
and we would share a future
                    full of hope and laughter.

Tante Marie: Her Sheltered Existence

She had a way of making me cringe,
Tante Marie of the Wagnerian bearing,
the majestic posture that belittled me
when I came into her presence.
I, awkward teen-age dowdy visitor to the villa—
she, always impeccably groomed and dressed,
each wrinkle adjusted by a harassed seamstress.
When she pointed at my bitten nails,
a safety-pinned strap, crookedly parted hair,
when she compared me with a hated cousin,
sleek sophisticated Laura of my own age,
I despaired of ever measuring up.

A lifetime later, a relative wrote that
she visited Tante Marie in a fancy clinic.
She found her strangely shrunken with age,
a fraction of the former Walkuere, but still
beautifully gowned, no hair out of place,
smiling graciously—without recognition,
remembering none of us, not even Laura.
Busily tearing up little pieces of paper
with dainty manicured fingers, she put
them into her mouth to nibble with relish.
The nurse said it could do no harm
and kept her content. I cringed.

Reconciliation at a Wedding

During their long estrangement when they met
by accident, both looked the other way
unwilling to acknowledge interplay
between two brothers, trying to forget
each had a share in every bygone debt
accumulated long ago. The day
resentments burst like flames, they swore to stay
apart for good, dense pride their safety-net.

As decades passed, as years became a gift
more valued with each subtle warning sign,
a wedding gathered them into one place
where love pervaded all, to melt, to lift
the outworn anger, and at last align
two fading men who wore each other's face.

For My Son's Second Wedding Day

A second marriage is a second chance
to form a union with a lasting bond.
This is no hasty love after one glance
but harvest after growing deeply fond
of one another in a testing time
of several years. It is no frivolous dance —
this joining of two people in their prime.

A second marriage is a simple cure
for all the allergies of loneliness
of men and women who become mature
enough to know that life produces stress,
not daily bliss of youthful fairy tales,
a bubble that must burst at first duress.
Support may now be sure when fortune fails!

This second marriage is my fervent hope
for you, dear son! From now on, you may cope —
clear-eyed, not starry-eyed — starting once more
to make a home securer than before.

A Manmade Corsage

Leaving the chapel, I removed
the corsage of white roses I wore
reluctantly during the ceremony
celebrating an alien Christ
credited with arrangements
for this "holy" marriage.

I pinned it to my travel dress,
perversely, for the homeward flight.
Wholly preserved, refrigerated
several days to perpetuate pain,
it made a hole in fragile cloth.

Brushing against stiff petals,
inhaling still heavy perfume,
I realized too late
such bloom was never real.
That hollow whiteness
enhanced by attar of roses
had deceived me for a while . . .
unlike the artifice of a near-
white dress pretending innocence.

The Remarriage
RHYME ROYAL

Of course, they both assured him they were pleased
that he had found renewal of hope, although
it seemed too recent that their mother ceased
to be the gear that moved his life, a blow
they shared. Observing his initial show
of grief, they feared he could not long endure.
Now sudden haleness made them hate the cure . . .

They missed her, though deriving consolation
from their own homes of married unity.
Viewing their parents from this midlife station,
they saw one lung whose lobes were meant to be
joined to each other inextricably.
If fate snuffed out one partner's final breath,
the one still using air would gasp for death.

Could they forget such closeness? She gave more
to him than anyone else, a partner wooed
with undiminished ardor for two score
of years, children a treasured interlude
of sharing in such growth, her gift renewed.
She raised them gently, two tempestuous sons.
Later, she loved their wives and little ones.

Not even half a year! The table tops she tended
despite arthritic hands were still agleam.
And how she planned that all the colors blended
into her favorite subtle color scheme!
Her husband teased, but later would redeem
himself, once giving her a dressing-gown
to match the bedroom, flowered, in pink and brown.

When they were boys, she used to enter
their grades painstakingly into a book.
Late afternoons, the kitchen was the center
for gathering after school before she'd cook
dinner, with them perched in the breakfast nook
watching her fingers deftly mix and spread
thick buttercream on fragrant gingerbread.

The garden never wore such lavish bloom
till she thinned out the beds, no warning bells
to indicate the rot of lurking doom
that ate away the substance of her cells
soon after planting time. Despite bad spélls,
her confidence in life was eloquent
in healthy loam, her flowering testament.

Of course, they claimed that they were glad for him . . .
but could a man mount such an alien stage
with someone in such brief an interim,
the past allotted to a bygone page?
They smiled with robot lips concealing rage,
unwilling to accept a brand-new leaf
in their old family book. They needed grief.

He asked them both to choose some things before
the wedding, since they were his rightful heirs,
since she, his wife, might change the whole decor!
They cared for none of the conventional wares
but trinkets their own mother saved upstairs:
the diaries, the notes in her fine script,
the dressing-gown, before that room got stripped.

Outside, reviving countless garden-hours,
they made a mute resolve as if to please
her, digging up clumps of her favorite flowers
for transplantation—iris, peonies—

as their perennial bloom of memories.
(The flowered dressing-gown would fit one wife,
symbol of harmony, an ordered life)

Before they left, the two glanced at each other
remembering the scented afternoons
after long hours in school, watching their mother
make country rhythms with her pots and spoons
keeping the freezer full. Whistling false tunes,
small boys once more, they stole before they fled
her final batch of cream-topped gingerbread.

A Rushing of Her Seasons

Approved of by the university,
enrolled too early for her tender age,
she traded girlhood irretrievably.

Life loomed no longer dull as she was free
to learn at will, devouring page on page
approved of by the university.

A model student hastening a degree,
claiming all knowledge as her heritage,
she traded girlhood irretrievably.

How well disguised, by day mute misery,
the lack of peers, an adult stage
approved of by the university.

At night, she acted out her tragedy:
when isolation locked her in its cage,
she traded girlhood irretrievably.

In streets of anguish she found company
by offering her tenderness in rage . . .
approved of by the university,
she traded girlhood irretrievably.

With Wagner: Through Storm to Calm

Once Wagner was the idol of a girl
steeped early in his "endless melody",
as storms were slyly starting to unfurl
in *Meistersinger*-land, her Germany.
When storm troops marched, that world was terror-tossed;
symbol of dread, the fierce Wagnerian sound
of Berchtesgaden signaled holocaust,
a battle cry piercing her underground.

In a new land, she would emerge matured,
at peace one day to know the old elation
hearing the *Ring*, soaring past pain endured,
singing redemption and conciliation.
At last, she gave her long-withheld applause
to music — pure, unmarred by human flaws.

Elegy For the Victims
of the Holocaust from Worms

We are the remnants, unravelled and torn
from fabric once sturdy, a proud congregation.
We, the survivors, returned here to mourn
those others, the doomed ones. We seek consolation
in reviving their names, recording their end
on a tablet for new generations to view:
Whether relative, neighbor, stranger or friend,
each of these victims was from Worms — and a Jew.

Age learns accepting but never forgetting:
time is a healer though scars shall remain
as constant reminders, lest the callous be letting
bygones be bygones, lest they blot out the stain.
Who can imagine how six million perished
when even six hundred should stagger the mind?
Theirs are the names from a City they cherished —
this fraction our portion, forever enshrined.

Between Two Graves, a World Apart
RHYME ROYAL

Ending a life far from her native land
she stayed here though she came reluctantly
when Hitler's hordes determined she be banned
from living out her days in Germany.
Endangered at an age past seventy,
she fled to Bombay, harbored by her son,
the perilous voyage a phenomenon.

Sometimes, my uncle wrote, she liked to stroll
along the seawall where old ladies met
in shade of palm-trees, relishing her role
of oldest recent immigrant; and yet
unreconciled, unable to forget
immaculate Worms, site of her cherished home
with vistas toward the Rhine, its ancient Dome.

Late in the Forties on a New Year's Eve,
a cable came to say grandmother passed
peacefully on, taking her final leave
from slumber into death, relieved at last.
In India, bodies must be buried fast:
the following day they'd laid her in the ground.
Her soul, no doubt, was promptly homeward-bound . . .

. . . winging past Worms, to burial grounds for Jews
where all these years Isaac, her husband, lay
without her. That plot had been too much to lose
in life; in death displaced, bones wrenched away
from him to alien soil till Judgment Day . . .
Even her son left India. All alone
remained one grave, untended, overgrown.

We learned before my uncle had retired
he made arrangements for perpetual care;
custodians were paid, a "hamal" hired
to pull the weeds . . . but change was in the air
those years, and foreign residents soon were
no longer welcome. Hate locked the graveyard door.
Now, after thirty years, we reached this shore!

Here we began a long exhausting quest,
my husband no less anxiously than I,
traversing Bombay, trying our best
to find one grave. Someone suggested: "Try
the former synagogue; it's quite nearby!"
Like two detectives following each trail,
we kept on moving citing our tale.

A caretaker gave us our needed break:
collecting dues when he was still a boy
he used to know my uncle. Now he'd take
us to the proper people. He'd enjoy
helping! With hope ahead, grateful to employ
him as our guide, we braved the crowds and heat
covering what seemed like miles with throbbing feet.

He led us to the Jewish Agency
where ancient men considered our plight.
Their secretary joined us luckily,
the only one who knew the very site:
a cemetery kept along the right
of way of trains along some thoroughfare.
She, kindly soul, offered to take us there.

Next day, we ventured on the final ride
standing in doubt before a rusty gate.
A native keeper acting mystified

made Rachel, our friend, negotiate
until he seemed to understand. Our wait
was not yet over, as he did not know
where German Jews were buried long ago.

Much time was vainly spent trying to trace
those huddled graves, headstones by vandals wrecked.
At last, we found grandmother Rosa's place
among the scattered exiles of our race
and stood in silence, paying due respect.
Only her name below the weeds was clear . . .
The Indian and his helper hovered near.

With urgent motions managing to ask
the Parsi boy to scour the leaning stone,
we watched him scrub. It was no easy task
to loosen layers of grime till marble shone,
till we beheld what no one could have known:
Without a plan, by some peculiar fate,
we chanced to come on grandma's birthday date!

Not on the schedule of our world-wide tour
Bombay had been an accidental stop
where on arrival — though we were unsure
of dates and facts, almost resigned to shop
or see the sights — we felt an urge to drop
all mundane plans — to find this mound of earth,
our visit happening on her day of birth!

Unlikely, that another relative
would come some future year to seek her out.
The names still dear to us would not outlive
another generation. How could we doubt
soil would take over, heedless weeds would sprout?
We chose two perfect pebbles tenderly
to put to rest with stones in Germany.

II

Nature and Art Studies

Rondeau of Acceptance

Leaves must be falling early this year . . .
Summer seems to be ending too soon.
Shadows grow long in the afternoon
as poplars shiver the atmosphere.

We tremble that autumn is almost here
when our footprints will disappear
completely, when all too inopportune
leaves must be falling.

Let us accept that endings are near
and light new fires to persevere,
rekindling an inner honeymoon
with tenderness to keep us immune
from fear of cycles that commandeer
leaves must be falling.

Day of Deliverance

Late blizzard has imprisoned us
with all the musts on our lists.
No way to carry out the chores
dragged in from yesterdays.
Rebellion is no use.
We acquiesce.
Even mail must wait.

We find sufficient food
on freezer shelves to cross
the market trip off our list
and have a feast.
We talk and rest; make music, love,
as nature builds a barricade
around our simple nest.

Next day the snow has stopped,
melting with April speed,
and chores have melted down
miraculously, with lesser urgencies
to carry out.

Storm Damage Redeemed

The silver maple splintered with a cry
that shook the autumn air, crashed to the ground
a moment later, settled with a sigh
subsiding, cranium crushed, without a sound.
Leaves were still pointed gracefully like green
gesturing hands, alive above that form
lying inert, before they lost their sheen
dying to dirge of stillness after storm.

The ragged wound gaped white along the stump
beyond recovery from amputation:
the severed limbs, sawed, bundled in a clump
of firewood, a bitter winter's ration.
Now they shall feed a flame, begin rebirth
as ashes for return to April earth.

Three Haiku for New Spring

Birches are greening,
break from the white of winter;
dead branches lie black.

Yesterday our birth;
today we leave faint footsteps
snowed in tomorrow.

Lend me a sharp knife
to cut first pussywillows
ending the bleakness.

April Recoveries

After long illness I tackle our hill
learning to walk here all over once more,
gingerly putting one footstep before
the other, as air rushes inward to fill
my lungs to the spilling point. Standing still
for a while, I feel how muscles restore
their pull to limbs that respond to the core
with a lift for the laggard will.

After long illness, our hill is my goal
for addressing the world in an April breeze,
caressing fresh branches on willow trees,
lamenting where winter has taken its toll.
My labor is needed! I crave my old role
as breath comes lighter, stiff bones start to ease.
Spring shall be healing all hurt, all disease,
letting humans in hope become whole.

A Gift of Freedom
from Dandelions

No longer encumbered by property
passing strange lawns, in a surge of surprise
I find new stirrings of spring in me.

I fondle the bold embroidery
of golden dandelions with eyes
no longer encumbered by property.

Viewed on our land without sympathy,
they meant weeds to combat, chores to despise.
I find new stirrings of spring in me

as I move along paths that are trouble-free,
as I follow the whim of butterflies,
no longer encumbered by property.

Without obligations, fresh energy
is a sudden gift that intensifies:
I find new stirrings of spring in me!

All flowers are mine, impartially
like sunshine and showers from April skies.
No longer encumbered by property,
I find new stirrings of spring in me.

Spring Cleaning

At dawn of another springtime
past seasons of turmoil were over,
when she would not remember their splendor
nor the name of one who had shared them.
And she emptied all her vases,
discarded cherished arrangements,
now brittle, dismally withered . . .
and briskly dismissed having gathered
such perishable shimmer
in an irretrievable summer.

Gypsy Moths

Sly like unseen rain
hissing in poplars and oaks,
in maples and aspens,
armies of caterpillars
immune to last year's poisons
devour tremulous leaves
leaving only spidery outlines
on bony branches.

Nature has struck back
for wanton meddling with
her subtleties; sprays
no longer a solution.
The red-spotted creatures
crawl slimily on, feast
on long suspension bridges
of treetops stripping
them winter-naked.

The scourge of June gardens,
soon they will swarm —
brown-winged gypsy moths
that hover on whitish females
that lay dormant masses of eggs
in ominous patches on trunks,
that produce fatter specimens,
that will be greedy for next
year's green of a helpless world.

Summer Chill in New Mexico

As we descend
after monotonous tan
of the West Mesa;
after the wide band of
Albuquerque's panorama,
eyes are pulled upward
to the surprise of a
sudden slate-colored rise—
these Sandia Mountains.

Waiting in the hot wind,
wherever I stand
nerve ends are drawn
to this massive shape,
its heaviness accentuated
by the wide dish of desert,
the huge ceiling of sky.

No gentle foothills
here to prepare me
for such sheer steepness.
No compromise.

A Shock of Green

After desert days
the amazing greenness
of my City reaches up
as we touch down,
tufts of green even
breaking through the
concrete of sterile
runways.

Maligned New York is
all summer lushness
like occasional perfect
loving late in life,
a surprise gift from
unpredictable Gods.
To have been away
makes it greener.

The Lone Ascent

Where curves of virgin forest slant unbroken
with single trees still emerald-edged below,
we turn to face the yellow-green of lichen
covering initial rocks where we must go.
Even the undergrowth is sparser here
but, bracing storms, evolved a strong design.
Now final boulders beckon to us, bare
beyond the last trace of the timberline.
The world recedes . . . No need of ornament
where every climber makes his lone ascent.

May Some Islands Dream Awhile

A world apart from one we know
in Southeast Asia's yesterday
islands keep dreaming, slow to grow.

Here gentle people come and go
content with dalliance and delay,
a world apart from one we know.

Where movement is adagio,
life-stilled five times for pause to pray,
islands keep dreaming, slow to grow.

Few visitors arrive to show
their know-how speed the Western way
a world apart from one we know.

The natives smile and bow although
in fathomless deep the eyes convey
islands keep dreaming, slow to grow.

May progress wait for natural flow;
may foreign greed fail to betray
a world apart from one we know.
Islands, keep dreaming, slow to grow!

Motion and Emotion: Tokyo to Kyoto
A SEDOKA SEQUENCE

BIG CITY
Tokyo takes time
to attune to, an ant heap
of organized commotion —
people, cars, subways
all moving most precisely,
a surprise of planned order.

TRAFFIC PROBLEMS
Beyond urban sprawl
caught in long lines of traffic
to celebrate a feast day,
throngs of calm drivers
move a car length at a time
toward mountain and beach ahead.

MOMENTS OF SERENITY
Along the wayside
small girls bring flowers to graves,
bent crones burn reverent incense,
commemoration
of summer-life that includes
all their dead on this weekend.

BEFORE THE BUDDHA
Men stop to marvel
before the great Daibutsu
enthroned in Kamakura —
immense bronze Buddha
with pensive fingers folded,
dwarfing the mountains in back.

THE BUDDHA'S STORY
His house blew away
in a typhoon of the past,
but no harm came to Buddha!
Again, patient crowds
in line, scurrying like ants
to buy cards in the courtyard.

RESPITE AT LAST
Lake of Hakone:
long queues wait to be carried
on languid steamer across
to the native inn
where hot baths unknot cramped limbs,
cool kimonos caress them.

SUCH SPEED!
Next day, *shinkansen*
the bullet-like train stuns us,
makes villages blur away,
woods vanish too fast
after the slow processions,
after the leisurely stops.

ANCIENT CITY
In old Kyoto
calm comes to stirred emotions.
The moment stops in motion.
At the poets' shrine
remembering the Buddha,
we surrender to stillness . . .

A Study of L's Work

L
is
not
tall
but L
paints
figures
as light
as no one
else. They
linger in a
languid pose
all elongated

O
we
see
long
limbs
convey
sublime
works of
lassitude
the people
lolling lax
idle as gods
in a colorful
world of clear
blue and yellow
lilting red full
of leisurely life
in limp loveliness
on hills of delight

For Muriel Rukeyser

On the way to join in the last tribute
to you, Muriel, as I take a late train
from my suburb to your cherished New York,
I think of you, sister poet, born in
my birth-year, recalling our final encounter:

Privileged to introduce you, I waited
along with a large audience. The last
possible moment you materialized
arriving in our town hall on your own,
a capricious cape around your shoulders
poorly concealing recent frailty.
We wondered why no one brought you.

Taking a firm stance, thin legs in flat shoes,
you swept us into the reading, filling the air
with passion and compassion, strong, for one hour.
You were hitting us where we lived too complacently.
Inscribing your last book for me later,
you spelled my name correctly without prompting.
(Not many do!) I took you to the train.
Why didn't I drive you all the way home?

Back in the present, again on the train, I return
along the same route you traveled that day.
After hearing close friends revive you in fragments,
after the shock of seeing you alive on film,
I bury myself in a paperback of Emily Dickinson's poems
that manage to console me more. She died in '86.
A hundred years from now, Muriel, the unborn
will read your poems on trains of the future
for consolation. You will rouse the complacent ones.

Villanelle for a Beloved Poet

She gave me a rose on Poetry Day
before I went back where I promised to be,
the scent surrounding my homeward way.

How well I knew that I could not stay
due to demands of a family.
She gave me a rose on Poetry Day,

its thorns reminding me to obey
my conscience, to conquer the notion to flee.
The scent surrounding my homeward way

conjured up a mysterious array
of thornless roses in memory . . .
She gave me a rose on Poetry Day

that turned into a wiltless bouquet
from the merciful Muse of Poetry,
the scent surrounding my homeward way.

No one may dwell, forever free,
in ivory towers of fantasy.
She gave me a rose on Poetry Day,
the scent surrounding my homeward way.

Annual Convention: Eating Your Words

The taste that jades my mouth during the journey home
is left from all the clashing foods consumed
served up by poets at convention time.
I would not mind the tentative, the timid flavors
of those not sure yet of the finite recipe,
nor did I spurn the newly boastful cook—
first prize! first recognition!—who may learn in time
to sweep the honors up like random crumbs
that have not formed a definite crust so far.

But, oh, how I regurgitate a constant fare
of annual egos ever on the fire
assaulting fresh arrivals with the brashest scent
from samples of their overcooked concoctions
(though after all these years one comes to know
the perpetrators by their stride and stridency,
like salesmen harking tidbits on a market aisle.
One ducks before the pitch but may get cornered;
then one smiles with artificial sweetener added,
swallowing all the gall.)
                                    Escape lies somewhere else.
The taste that shall delight after the journey home
will linger long after I rinse my mouth, erase
unpleasant aftertastes. It will derive
from unexpected snacks throughout those days—
refreshing, unpretentious, some without a flaw,
serving as needed seasoning for my own modest menu.
Despite our consciousness of limitations,
a few of us could feast, compare ingredients,
sharing the challenge of elusive goals.

Birth Pangs of a New Sonnet

Leave, dream, before I venture to invent
a sonnet of my own, a form to start
with poet-singers long before I came —
Petrarch and Dante, gods to me who lent
unfailing ear and tongue to this our art,
followed by greats of such immortal name
as Spencer, Shakespeare, Milton, Keats — I blame
you, dream, and must entreat you to depart
lest I might step where no mere earthlings tread.
You dare me, aiming such a wily dart
into my veins that blood turns turbulent
pulsing in feverish wonder why fate led
me here . . . Have I by choice inherited
that legacy? Am I your instrument?

So be it! Let me move in tune with you,
bold dream that brings fresh purpose to my days
with rhythms meeting in a novel dance.
Unable to resist, I seek my cue
between the lines of tensions, interplays
of music not imagined in advance
found, flawless, at their birth as if by chance,
as if you, dream, had brought to life old ways
to build upon, superimposed on me.
Rhymes, unrehearsed, chime sonnet roundalays
of interwoven song, tradition-new,
a subtle form of modern masonry
left in my wake, willed to posterity —
humbly submitted for a fair review.

How well I know this heritage will bring
me more than the fulfillment of a dream:
rough rocks of hardship will obstruct the road
where jealousy may lurk, its wasp-like sting
hampering my stride. Uncouth hordes may scheme
to undermine my pride, besmirch my code,
and would-be poets of an alien mode
will ridicule the dream, scorn and blaspheme
all sonnet forms. Yet I am undeterred
to labor far from chains of academe;
nor shall I stoop to heed the badgering
of tone-deaf men, who—even if they heard
the music of the gods—would be unstirred.
Though I may weep, my sonnet, dance and sing!

My Inviolate Land
A MALAYAN PANTOUM

On a distant planet alone
strange beings beckoned to me
in a place I had always known
in the mind's hidden history.

Strange beings beckoned to me
beneath a cathedral of palms
in the mind's hidden history:
I followed them without qualms.

Beneath a cathedral of palms
I knew all the words that were sung.
I followed them without qualms
now using the native tongue.

I knew all the words that were sung
no earthling would understand,
now using the native tongue
in this inviolate land.

No earthling would understand
I felt a fierce need to stay
in this inviolate land—
Did I venture that sojourn one day?

I felt a fierce need to stay
in a place I had always known.
Did I venture that sojourn one day
on a distant planet alone?

III

*The New Arithmetic
of Love and Friendship*

Geometry of Love

The lines of love would not be hard to draw
if all would run in one direction, straight
from start to end. Some deviate, unsure
of any course; some, tangled, heed no law
entwining others; some terminate
too early with a fading signature.
Advancing years have seen our love endure
through many trials . . . erase, obliterate
all obstacles, leaving this unity.
May vigorous strokes prevail, defying fate
as life draws late designs. We trace in awe
two lines converged for good in harmony
and pray to let them soar triumphantly
to heights in worlds beyond without a flaw.

Two Learned Loving
A TWELVE-LETTER LYRIC

Wedding over,
two living alone
on a ledge in wide water
in a land never at war—
we learned love anew
on a golden noon
in lingering wind
and even in rain.

Avid to dare, never too tired,
we went riding a road
along a ridge, over wall;
went wading a wave
at evening tide;
went nearer toward all
waving a wand to
deliver elation on a wing.

We learned love, an old art,
and we earned glad rewarding.
In leaving, we leaned
well over too long
till land reverted
to a dot on a wave.
Later we longed in vain to go
and never to leave again.

Breaking Through His Sound Barrier

Excitement has mounted all morning
with startling discoveries:
"My shoes — how they clatter on tile —
this paper crackles so crisply!
The dishes — they rattle — they clang —
and the phone rings the chandelier!"

His spirit on high starts to sing:
"O I hear my own voice so clearly!
I listen, the first time in years
to pick up your slightest whisper,
the chuckle, my dear, that is yours!"

This tiny hearing device
vibrates with wonder for him —
a small boy again who has found
in old age the delights he has missed:
a new world made sounder by science,
his old world that revels in sound.

Love be a Shield
PANTOUM

As our span runs out,
signs are no longer clear.
Day breaks with rays of doubt;
night wears a cloud of fear.

Signs are no longer clear
in dread we may be parted.
Night wears a cloud of fear
unless we are lion-hearted.

In dread we may be parted
we care more consciously;
unless we are lion-hearted
age is drab company.

Where mutual joy is past,
day breaks with rays of doubt.
Love be a shield to last
as our span runs out.

My Sonnet is a Subterfuge

These lines, unspoken, have no other goal
than giving vent to pressures on the mind
in sonnets seeking what I cannot find
in ordinary speech, strict form the sole
free interchange allowed. Would I extol
your powers to your face and dare unbind
a tongue used to restraint, to the confined
words of a woman tutored in control?

My sonnets are a symptom, not a cause—
and though aware of it, we keep dissecting
the form as art, all meaning under covers.
Then, we are safe to speak of it, to pause
and gaze at paper-love, meanwhile erecting
barriers between two poets, would-be lovers.

Dear Amy

The incidents of love are more than its events—
Investment's best expositor is the minute per cents
                                    —Emily D. 1914

DEAR AMY: I am glad you wrote
when you sent me your invitation
that it's raining again in your state.
It is how I remember ominous Ohio.
It revives a rained-out washed-out
cried-out rendezvous with a poet
the gist of his work of great worth
the rest of him not worthy enough
and I not worldly enough though
old enough to weep for better causes,
all of Cleveland a hostile blur
as I watched incredulous stunned
as he kissed fondled other women
after a stunning performance
quite unaware I had come to him
for more than a mere affair.
Later he lured me to give in
to new promises of clearing
as Lake Erie lured me to give way
to a skyscraper grief from my window
surely to give poetry up for good.
In time I gave up falling in love
with poets to give myself wholly
properly to their poems. Next year
I'll read my own poetry in Ohio
and get rid for good of that ghost.
Thank you for asking me to come.

Villanelle in Praise of Elizabeth,
No Saint

They call her Lisa for her special smile
of hints provocative yet innocent
relishing life in unconventional style.

For anyone hurt she walks the extra mile
supporting those who stumble, sorrow-bent:
they call her Lisa for her special smile.

Uneasiness walked with her down the aisle
when she was wed, who would prefer a tent
relishing life in unconventional style.

On luxury streets, she could not reconcile
herself to callousness. The husbands came and went.
They call her Lisa for her special smile,

the generous mouth, its language without guile
sending the message gifts were to be spent,
relishing life in unconventional style.

This is no Mona Lisa, smiling while
denying urges ever turbulent.
They call her Lisa for her special smile
relishing life in unconventional style.

Rondeau for a Friend
With an Unalterable Schedule

You are my friend . . . You justify
your absence like a butterfly
so busy dipping down all day,
you find no time to stop, to stay
a while without some alibi.

When I am home, please, tell me why
we rarely meet, fond eye to eye,
though letters vouch, when I am away,
you are my friend?

To make us laugh, grant us to cry
together, let us not deny
our need for touching to convey
warmth of these words without delay:
You are my friend!

Behind Barriers of Global Communication

There are so many words we never say
for fear of laying bare our frailty
although the hour is nearing judgment day.

"Please, bear with me a while. I lost my way" —
a simple phrase, a would-be remedy.
There are so many words we never say!

We fail to touch; we shun true interplay
doling out measured love by slow degree
although the hour is nearing judgment day.

"I bear no falsehood. Trust me, friend, I pray."
The cry is silent. Posing publicly,
there are so many words we never say.

If only human voices could convey
our real needs! Pride chokes the desperate plea
although the hour is nearing judgment day.

No hindsight compensates for love's delay
as we approach our common destiny.
There are so many words we never say
although the hour is nearing judgment day.

Testament

No one but you I trust to weed
my prized perennial bed,
no other I could find to feed
songbirds with frost ahead.
There's no one else I'd give the key
to straighten out this room,
sort papers, poems kept by me,
save plants that rarely bloom.
No other would take pains to match
the fabric for new drapes . . .
and no one else would care to patch
family wounds and scrapes.
Some future day, I know I must
leave cherished work undone —
You share my loves. You have my trust,
wife of my first-born son!

IV

The Humanities:
Tests and Finals

I, Walt Whitman, Listening

I hear America sighing, the various complaints I hear;
Those of the workers, each one sighing long hours, low wages;
Those of the jobless sighing that welfare does not well enough;
The sighs of the rich that their assets are shrinking;
The sighs of the middle-class feeling squeezed from all sides.
The politicians are sighing about voters' indifference;
The voters, they sigh that politicians are corrupt.
The old sigh about the young taking too many liberties;
The young are sighing for more freedom.
The women's sighs deplore discrimination;
The men keep sighing for a vanished vision of women.
The black sigh that they have gained too little, too slowly;
The white sigh because the black continue their sighs.
And at night, the sudden sigh of fear in the dark,
When violence stalks young and old, great and humble,
Men and women, rich and poor, black and white;
Everyone sighing, complaining, no longer singing;
And I, Walt Whitman, listening and missing
The strong melodious songs of joy in America.

Slum Story

Above the drone of the evening news
the nightly crying dies to a whimper.
They shrug it off unwilling to tamper
with a neighbor's concerns.

Next morning, the shame.
Aghast at the burns
along the frail frame
of the half-naked boy,
they offer ointment . . .
candy . . . a soda . . . a toy . . .

"How did it happen?" The answer, too quick:
"I played with matches. I burned my back."
The eyes are searing holes in his face
full of fearful knowledge:

There is no place
to hide from the man
in his mother's bed
who hits and burns him,
wants him dead.
The grimmest hurt
as he suffers abuse —
the mother keeps watching
the evening news.

Shopping Trip

After a day of ungracious living
I drove away from impertinent clerks,
indifferent cashiers and other rude operators,
out of tune with the age of my children.
"In our day" (I never meant to use that phrase)
we said "thank you" and "please" even
if at times we did not care either.
Heading home
heeding directions EXACT CHANGE LANE,
I drove along dropping my coins
into the faceless mouth of the toll booth.
And then, for the first time that day,
I was treated courteously.
A green light flashed, promptly,
in large letters: THANK YOU!
You are welcome indeed, I sang out,
grateful for small favors.

Ballade of the Lad
at the Promising Sea

At high tide of his youth when he dreamed to be grown,
all his fancies were beamed on a turbulent sea
with the wind in his face on a ship of his own
as he braved the huge breakers exuberantly.
And his ship would respond at last setting him free,
for no surer-eyed captain had sailed it before;
special stars would be guides toward a destiny
to a point of great promise ahead on the shore.

In the middle of life there were worries and debts;
still he found a retreat by the sea every year,
and he learned in a storm how a sailor forgets
going home some rough day, lets his wake disappear—
but he always returned reinforced against fear
to resume any cargo, with stars to restore
early faith in the course he was destined to steer
to a point of great promise ahead on the shore.

When the ebb of his living showed plainly in sight,
he perceived that most dreams were not meant to come true,
but the knowledge his stars would outlast any night
lent endurance to days with his seascape in view.
With the undertow conquered, without compass, he knew
to cast anchor at last, too becalmed to explore
unknown stretches of sea, distant patches of blue
to a point of great promise ahead on the shore.

On the ultimate voyage, he would choose a canoe
for a daring departure, his final encore—
he would shove off to sea with "ahoy" and "adieu"
to a point of great promise ahead on the shore.

The Pocketknife
GLOSA

"The Years of youth are rich in lessons learned . . .
Too often early knowledge will be spurned
later when our elders' backs are turned . . .
till we become the parents, all-concerned."

His father taught him how to use a knife,
that first small pocketknife he let him own
urging him to remember all through life
that knives are never meant to settle strife,
intended for domestic tasks alone.
The father was a carpenter who earned
his living through his skill, the cornerstone
for family needs. He of his flesh and bone
paid little heed till later he discerned
the years of youth are rich in lessons earned.

Dad showed him why he should not draw a blade
toward his chest but pointed carefully
away; to keep it handy, undisplayed
but always sharp, for dull blades often made
unwanted cuts. It was a theory
he never needed much where he sojourned,
until one day he owned an ailing tree
and cut the deadwood out — disastrously —
then realized, as disinfectant burned,
too often early knowledge will be spurned.

In time, he got the news his father died,
a bag of small possessions left by him
back in the hospital. He finally cried
finding the pocketknife kept at his side,

blades razor-sharp, still fit to make a shim,
open a box, or sharpen pencils. He yearned
to see him once again, to watch him trim
a shingle, or strip a sucker limb by limb.
Regrets are live, with the remains inurned,
later when our elders' backs are turned.

Roles now reversed, a father all too soon,
he tries to hand down lessons, stoops to preach
too often with the hour inopportune,
lacking the patience of the man, rough-hewn,
whose pocketknife he carries. Memory would reach
across the space where he adjourned
to listen deep to that deliberate speech:
"Slow down. You move too fast. The way to teach
is by example" . . . The mill of time has churned
till we become the parents, all-concerned.

Amputee on the Beach

The hospital behind, recovering on this shore,
his missing leg not hurting any more
except at secret moments none must share . . .
on such a morning as he sits to stare
beyond his sheltered terrace to the sea,
a random bird darts from dense shrubbery . . .

Brown, undistinguished, till he sees the bare
stump of a missing leg tremble on air,
until he recognizes with a start
one like himself, his feathered counterpart
who teeters, picking morsels off the breakfast tray,
twitters and lingers long, then soars away.

"You little bird, why did you come to me,
your leg like mine cut off below the knee?
You make the best of it and, quite a sport,
balance the rest of life on one support!
Small friend-in-need, you still can hop and fly
around this splendid earth. And so will I."

Small Pickings

Only a matter of manners
ever made her mad at him —
the voice booming too brashly
in public places, unrestrained
sneezes exploding in church
to make people snigger, and
particularly the picking
of teeth anywhere, any time,
with the little wooden sticks
he collected in all pockets.

She loved him deeply, no doubt
about it, though she tried
to change such habits for fifty
years, steadfastly picking on him.
She loved his warm voice, admired
his self-confident stance,
even his indifference to proper
appearances; yet she pulled away
when he hugged her in public.

Now the voice has been stilled;
a sneeze of any volume would be
welcome in the lasting silence.
She sorts out clothing for her
charitable groups and collects —
from pants and jackets, from
the red hunting coat, the green
bathrobe, even the flannel pajama
tops last worn, laundered in haste
without checking the breast pocket —

a heap of toothpicks lovingly,
carefully accumulating them still
in their pristine white wrappers,
now smiling tolerantly through
blurred glasses upon the kindling
for her private pyre.

Of Birth and Death on a Kibbutz
PASTORAL

At last, the nights were calm beyond the fence
surrounding acres salvaged from the swamps,
now home for former refugees who fled
from lands of lifelong persecution once.
The children who were born on this Kibbutz
were made secure in nightly shelters where
they never saw the stars above the valley
nor sudden lightning bolts from hostile shells
across the borderlines of Lebanon.
Now Miriam was happy all through night
though Jaakov still kept watching at his post
and never taking safety here for granted.
This season, she could hear the soothing sound
of gentle breathing come from three-year-olds —
Naomi and Shoshannah near at last,
a miracle of domesticity
come true beyond the cruel years of war,
the stealthy kind that threatened every night.

Ten years ago, her husband said to her:
My dear, it's time before we get too old . . .
we should have children soon to carry on
when we are gone, but Miriam looked at him,
his graying temples, the work-worn body
supported by the artificial leg,
the good one carrying the greater share
in weary hours serving as a guard.
She only said: How can we bring a child
into this woeful world, so worrisome
for Jews as well as for the whole of mankind?

And Jaakov turned more taciturn than ever
and felt twice crippled then. Before the blast
that took his leg, he was a lusty lad
who eagerly took arms defending lands
and lives of Israel. Now he performed
his nightly watch for danger from the dark,
alerting other men to manly tasks.

Though passion sometimes flared between those two,
Jaakov was sure of Miriam's firm resolve
of childlessness and never brought it up.
It seemed a miracle that made her pregnant
when both were middle-aged, and even more
when Miriam got so huge she saw a doctor
in Tel Aviv who said: You carry twins!
How strange that now she was quite reconciled
to bringing children into hazards here.
It was the will of God . . . so she rejoiced.
And he was happy, too. He brought fresh milk
each morning from communal cows for her.
The other wives took on her chores; they churned
the butter, made the cheese and gathered eggs
to feed the one who ate and drank for three,
and all said prayers when she began her labor.
Another miracle then came to pass,
the midwife said. She had an easy time.

She had an easy time despite her age,
despite the size of full-developed babies.
And then, despite the ever-present danger
from snipers' bullets, death from sneak attacks,
they had become a close-knit family.
The mother nursed, another miracle,
those strutting breasts with such abundant milk!

Each evening before the dangerous dark,
compulsory shelter-time for little ones,
the four spent hours alone, their daily harvest
of sharing gratefully their simple meals.
Moreover, lately, as the troops began
to enter Lebanon to end the threat
that had been constant for the past decade,
the nights were calm beyond the fence at last,
and soon the babies were allowed to stay
above the ground, sweet huddles in their cribs,
with cows now softly lowing lullabies.

Thus weeks had passed in strange tranquillity
until one morning-sun of horror rose . . .
when all, around the television set
in the communal hall, would witness scenes
of death and cruel destruction in two camps . . .
such scenes so well recalled from former days,
the blood-baths of their past, to make them cringe
in shame, with outrage, full of sudden pity.
Was this the price extracted now for safety?
It was too high a price to pay, to watch
these helpless people slaughtered in Beirut,
to feel the guilt of standing by alive!
Dead Arab children huddled where they slept
mowed down by phalangists, now caused response
from Miriam and Jaakov, Jewish settlers
once refugees as were those victims slain . . .
These two found shelter here to start new lives
among their own. How could they stay unmoved?

Enough of all the bloodshed, Jaakov cried.
And Miriam wept and held her babies tight.
Their new-found battle cry became *Peace Now*

along with thousands taking up the vow,
a challenge to all leaders bent on war.
They opened doors to tend to refugees
who soon would flee across the border here.
They opened hearts to kindred families
to bind their wounds, to still each other's fear.
Where monsters of distrust had lurked before,
a calmness spread beyond the open door.

Departures

So many going
when days turn gray
with cold winds blowing
the frail away.

Coping with Losses
A SEQUENCE OF MASON SONNETS

A NATURAL LAW

Watching the ways of various widowed friends,
we stand in awe before the bravery
of some of them who manage to revive
after their period of mourning ends.
With pity we observe the agony
of others stumbling onward half alive
after their loss, who never even strive
for new supports. Withering, a severed tree
cannot be saved; leaves, lifeless without hope.
For such, their years are wasted wantonly,
spent unaware what natural law intends —
to feel the ebb and flow of life, to grope
far down toward roots, absorbing sun, to cope
with elements, become a tree that bends.

RECUPERATION

With spring this year, emergence of a friend
from bleakness is a miracle, her stance
a triumph of life . . . Widowed years ago,
she was a tree uprooted by the end
of marriage, wrenched by hurricane-advance
of dread disease. Beyond initial blow,
past normal mourning-time, the undertow
of her despair lurked in each utterance
until this season could produce new shoots
from lifeless wood, spreading a radiance
of leaf-green hope . . . Assured now she can bend
under a storm, preserve resilient roots
for second growth and fruit, she substitutes
despondency with joy, spring's dividend.

COMPENSATIONS

A new relationship late in our lives
brims with surprises of a sudden gift
falling like unexpected desert rain
into diminished soil. As it arrives
we breathe more easily, sensing a lift
in every bone, the secret seats of pain;
that instant feel invincible again
instead of facing years barely adrift
on memories alone. The friends we lost
though irreplaceable, now subtly shift
into one strange composite that survives.
New currents lave the sand forestalling frost
leaving deep marks where our pathways crossed,
a found oasis where fresh friendship thrives.

We watch the ways of men and women, ill,
in pain, who know their days are limited,
and humbly bow before the steadiness
in human beings of such iron will,
such strength we all shall need. Others, instead,
cringe before death and cause increased distress
to those they must soon leave. Though pitiless
and self-concerned, weak on their final bed,
they will be mourned, albeit with relief
when all is over, when the survivors shed
those awful memories. O to lie still
and calm, assured our suffering will be brief,
to spare our dear ones bitterness in grief,
leaving warm memories nothing can kill!

Rising as we arrived, the gracious host
as ever through the long decades we shared
from heights to valleys, he put us at our ease
though lately in appearance like a ghost
of his young mountain self. Relieved, we dared
to chat and laugh without restraint, to please
our friend ignoring the malignancies
of fate. He poured the wine, aware we cared
and felt like grieving, yet honoring his cue
performing naturally. Nobody stared
at limbs like ropes as he stood up to toast
friendship; and as he locked the door, we knew
that we had brought one needed gift in lieu
of flowers — one hour of lives in life engrossed.

His mother roused him with her urgent call
to fetch the violin she used to play
in concert halls of grandeur long ago.
Reluctant, he complied, afraid to stall
too long; with dread preparing what to say
if crippled fingers would not hold the bow
or if the mind, long in adagio,
had lost the passages to yesterday.
Amazed, he watched his mother now transcend
all former triumphs, holding without dismay
her instrument wrapped in its Chinese shawl . . .
She stroked it, whispering: "Good-bye, old friend!",
an inner ear attuned to hear the end
with encores scheduled in the greatest hall.

The poet sure her final year on earth
is come, aware she has no time to lose,
works without pause, labors undauntedly
toward a climactic song, weighing the worth
of yet another book, aiming to choose
the best, the gist of life. With poetry
claiming her like a fever, she heeds no plea
to save her energy, brooks no excuse
for laying down the pen until she basks
in pure accomplishment, true to the Muse.
Convinced her life's companion in his dearth
of action after grief will welcome tasks
to fill the void ahead, at last she asks:
Please, publish this for me, for my rebirth.

What is a Happy New Year?
SESTINA FOR 1985

Once more, a year is coming to its end
when humans mark a new unsullied leaf
with resolutions to improve their ways,
with hopes and expectations for the span
that is as yet unknown, shrouded ahead,
and when they wish each other happiness.

The aging process changes terms of happiness:
we who are moving closer to the end
along life's book, plan not too far ahead,
content to turn the pages leaf by leaf,
grateful for health in our allotted span,
eager to witness days in novel ways.

Our children, center of the book, find ways
to celebrate their mid-life happiness
including their own young, whose ages span
the teen-age years. For some, they will soon end
though adulthood still seems beyond belief;
some, children yet, are imprints glimpsed ahead.

The new year brings new worries for a head
of such a family who seeks the ways
and means to help each child, a separate leaf
in ledgers saved for all. Mixed happiness
and grief intrude, as parents dread the end
of school years, treasuring this final span.

The youngest members of the family span
the years without a qualm, forging ahead

with utter trust that time will never end
for them who cannot guess the various ways
their elders would define as happiness —
carefree, they now remove this calendar leaf.

the ones who can sustain a strong belief
nothing on earth would be the final span,
are nurturing a secret happiness.
They see a shining volume lie ahead,
the pages pure, marked in mysterious ways
for every soul, in glory without end.

There is an end inherent in each leaf,
but soon renewal outweighs death, each span
assuring life ahead . . . toward happiness.